the
American
Chameleon

the American Chameleon

William White Jr., Ph.D.

STERLING NATURE SERIES

STERLING PUBLISHING CO., INC. NEW YORK

Oak Tree Press Co., Ltd.
London & Sydney

OTHER BOOKS BY THE SAME AUTHOR

The Angelfish: Its Life Cycle

Earthworm Is Born

Edge of the Pond

Forest and Garden

Frog Is Born

The Guppy: Its Life Cycle

The Siamese Fighting Fish: Its Life Cycle

Terrarium in Your Home

Turtle Is Born

The author and publisher wish to thank James M. White and Elizabeth J. White for their work in maintaining the herd of anoles studied in this book; William White III for special optical apparatus and Rebecca L. White for preparing the manuscript.

CONTENTS

Illus. 1. A large male sleeps in the sun, eyes closed, with his head resting on a large leaf.

INTRODUCTION

The American chameleon or anole may well be the most popular pet lizard in the world. Hundreds of thousands are sold in pet shops and department stores every year. In many areas of the southern United States, these fascinating lizards are caught in almost any yard or woods. They make ideal pets, for they are easy to keep, do not require much space or exotic foods and will survive for many years with reasonable care.

Anoles are very adaptable little creatures and they will take advantage of man's habits as quickly as any animal. This is one of the keys to their abundance around human houses and other buildings. One aspect of this is their use of potted plants in which to lay their eggs. The author and his wife frequently found anole eggs neatly tucked into the potted plants to be taken into the house before the cold weather set in. Other North Carolina neighbors actually had some anoles hatch in their living rooms, where the potted plants were set in sunny, warm windows for the winter.

This book deals with the American chameleon from two points of view—first as an easily kept representa-

Illus. 2. The click of the camera shutter is enough to bring the anole to instant attention. It is this characteristic of extreme sensitivity that enables the anole to survive in its highly competitive environment.

tive of the reptile class and second as a very enjoyable pet. The American chameleon is an especially good species for observation in either the home or class-room.

1. BEHAVIOR

Anoles have many interesting habits in nature, most of which can also be noted in captivity. They will often spend much of the daylight hours quietly sunning themselves. It is understood that their bodies synthesize certain required biological chemicals, probably vitamins, with the aid of sunlight. Experiments show that they will seek out periods of direct exposure to the sun during which they display their brightest green coloring. However sluggish they may appear during these sunbaths, they are nonetheless wide awake and their senses are at peak efficiency (Illus. 1 and 2).

This ability to remain absolutely motionless and blend into the foliage stands them in good stead, since predators, including human beings, will pass them by without ever seeing them.

Defence of Territories

One of the most important aspects of the behavior of anoles is their defence of territories. While males do this instinctively and with great energy, females are less inclined to do so (Illus. 3 and 4).

Illus. 3. A male patrols his territory.

Males will often take over territories defined by some natural or man-made barrier such as a wall, a stream or an open area such as a lawn. They often remain in one spot within their territory, but if an interloper appears, they will immediately rush out with throat-flap extended and with head and body bobbing up and down as a signal to warn him off. Many large males will permit numbers of females about them, but will carry on displays with intruder males. If other

10

Illus. 4. A female rests on a green leaf while stalking insects. Note the delicate grip of the toes on the leaf.

males are introduced into the territory of an established male and his harem, the original occupants will open their mouths aggressively and try to drive the intruders out (Illus. 6).

The less dominant males will seek to hide especially at night since anoles do not see well in the dark and are nearly defenceless then.

Illus. 5. A female will often return to a specific leaf to rest or spend the night. Here a female (middle) beds down in one leaf fold where she will be nearly invisible from above.

Illus. 6. A large male on the left, with one of the females from his harem, protests the introduction of new individuals.

Illus. 7. A female in the "head-raised" threatening posture.

In captivity, dominant males will so bully the intruder males, driving them away from their food, that the latter will actually starve to death. While there are virtually no fights to the death, there are frequent battles in which the less dominant males suffer tail injuries. This protection of the territory involves constant patrol and takes more time than even the pursuit of food (Illus. 7 and 8).

Illus. 8. A large male surveys his hard-won territory. Note the torn skin and twisted tail, scars from territorial battles.

Feeding

The feeding actions of the anole involve three of its fundamental physical characteristics—its keen senses, its ability to climb and crawl and its lightning-quick reflexes. It will actually stalk a fly with slow, deliberate steps and snatch it right out of the air as it begins to fly away. However, its major food in its native environment—the southern United States—appears to be the cricket and the cockroach. The large anoles, male and female, pursue crickets into the soil or under plants with great agility (Illus. 9, 10, 11, 12, and 13).

14

Illus. 9. A large mature male senses the presence of a cricket.

Illus. 10. In a lightning-fast movement, the anole has seized the cricket.

Illus. 11. With a few twists of its head, the anole works the main part of the cricket into its jaws where it will be crushed by the rows of teeth.

Water Requirements

One of the major needs aside from insect or other animal protein is water. Studies have shown that the largest water loss from the anole does not take place from the lungs as with many other animals, but from the skin. The lungs themselves are rather simple and not overly divided to increase surface area. The loss of

16

Illus. 12. The cricket is completely down the throat of the anole with only its legs still protruding.

Illus. 13. The cricket is nearly engulfed, the anole looks in all directions, wary of anything that may have moved in too close.

Illus. 14. A mature female approaches a water droplet. Anoles drink by licking water drops from their surroundings.

water through the skin probably means that the anole breathes, that is, has gas exchange, through the skin in addition to the lungs. Anoles are therefore restricted to fairly damp environments.

While they resist heat and cold very well, anoles cannot resist drying out, or dessication, and will dig down into the moist soil or hide in the moist holes of dead trees during hot-dry spells. Anoles will not drink from a large water source such as a pond or stream. They usually drink by licking or lapping with the forepart of the tongue at drops of water such as raindrops on plants (Illus. 14).

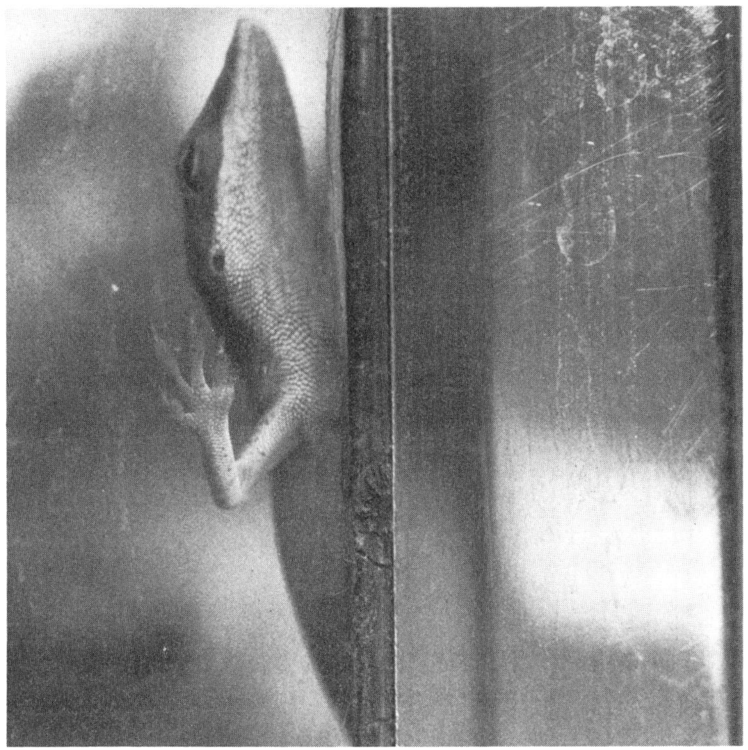

Illus. 15. An anole uses its adhesive-padded feet to climb up the glass of its enclosure and seek water drops.

Their ability to climb enables them to obtain a great deal of such water (Illus. 15).

The author often releases reptiles and amphibians into the plantings around his house in Pennsylvania. Since the winters are too cold for many species they are caught in the late summer and left to run loose in the study or greenhouse area for the autumn and winter.

This never ceases to amuse young visitors as much as it upsets adult ones. For several years the author has released anoles into the flower beds. Each season, one or more will discover that the garden hoses hung outside will drip water even when turned off. The small patches of plants under these drips become the most eagerly sought-after parts of the garden. Anoles scamper up plants and walls to get to the supply of water dripping from the hoses.

Hibernation

Anoles will crawl in almost anywhere to hibernate for the winter. They will make their way into cracks in walls, around doors of houses and garages, under window sills and almost anywhere else. They are frequently found in the heart of firewood logs. Many a time the author has uncovered sleeping, nearly unconscious, anoles in pieces of firewood he has split with an axe. Since they are in the soft spongy, usually rotted areas of the log, they usually escape injury. However, such anoles should not be brought into the house, but packed in bundles of straw and grass and put in a container, such as an open tin can. This container should be left out of doors, placed in a sheltered area.

If reptiles are heated up too fast from hibernation, their metabolism, which has slowed down with the cold, will begin working too fast and they will starve before they can waken enough to eat and digest food.

2. CARING FOR ANOLES IN CAPTIVITY

It is not difficult to keep anoles in captivity quite successfully if the following six rules are followed:

1. Do not place more than one male in an enclosure. The male, along with only two or three females, should occupy no less than 1,700 cm² (288 square inches) of space—equivalent to a terrarium 60 cm by 30 cm (2 feet by 1 foot).

2. Keep the bottom soil at least 10 cm (4 inches) deep and fill the terrarium with growing green plants in a moist environment. (Anoles do not do well with plastic flowers or cacti.)

3. Spray or squirt some moisture (clean, dechlorinated water) on the plants and the anoles every day.

4. Make sure the whole terrarium has a good cover of glass or sheet plastic. One edge may be slid back or raised just slightly to let in fresh air and let out trapped air each day during the warmest part of the day.

5. The terrarium must not be chilled and must be given no less than six hours of direct sun or strong incandescent light each day.

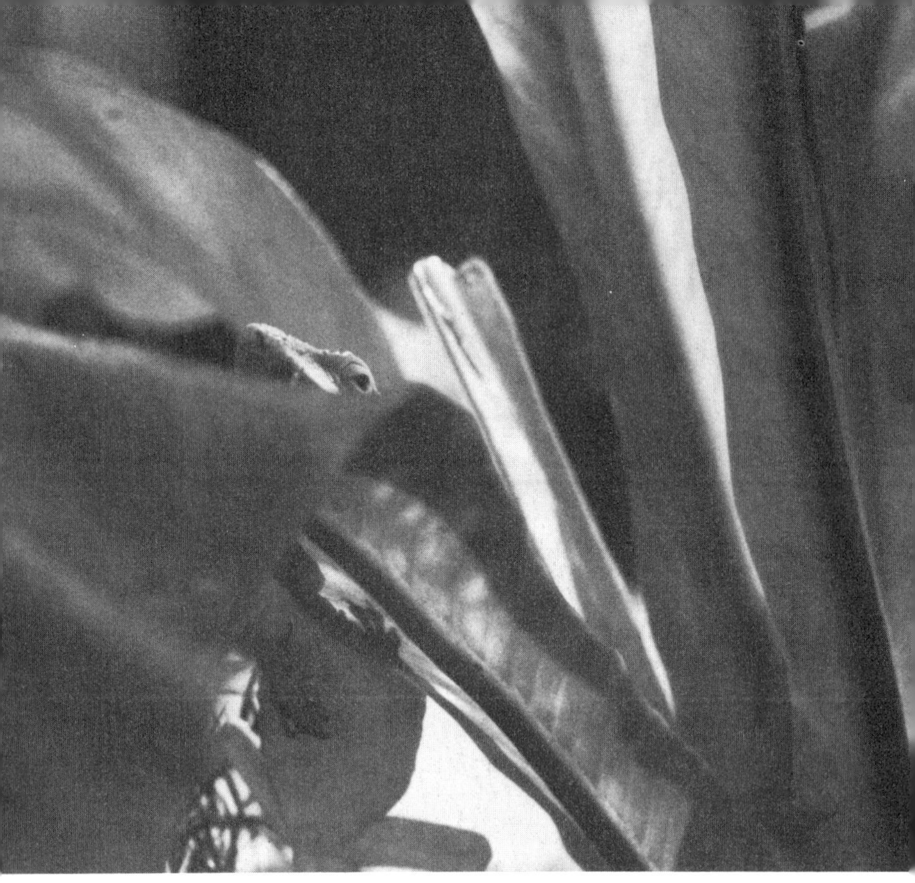

Illus. 16. As night settles, a large male beds down in a leaf fold with only his nose and eyes showing, to keep watch.

6. The anoles should be fed on live flies and larger insects such as crickets at least once a week. While mealworms, available at most pet supply houses, will suffice they are not good as the basic, permanent food.

3. FORM AND FUNCTION

The American chameleon is really not a chameleon at all, nor does it resemble the true chameleon of the Old World, apart from its ability to change color. The true chameleons, which are much larger lizards from Asia and Africa, belong to a different family. The American chameleon, which is really a small type of iguana, ranges across nearly the whole of the southern half of the United States from Colorado to the Carolinas. The scientific name of the most common species found in the United States and the one shown in this book is *Anolis carolinensis* subspecies: *carolinensis* and from this is derived its correct name, the anole, the name used throughout this book. The genus *Anolis* is very widely distributed throughout Central and South America and is especially abundant in the West Indies.

Anoles are easily distinguished from all other lizards by their grassy-green color, pink throat fan or "dewlap" and characteristic head shape (Illus. 17 and 18).

Anoles vary in size—some old males may reach 16.5 cm (6½ inches) in length but the average adult is about 10 cm (4 inches). Following the pattern of most

Illus. 17. A large male raises his head and looks about intently over his territory. The bulge under his chin at the back of the throat is the male dewlap.

vertebrates that depend on insects for their food, they are very protective of territories.

The anole is almost totally active during the day or, to put it another way, it is *diurnal* in habit. It blends well with the plants and trees of its woodland home. Like all reptiles, it is cold-blooded or *poikilothermous*, that is, its body temperature varies with the air temperature of its environment. Throughout the hot summer days it must constantly move from sunshine

24

Illus. 18. A mature female hunts for food among the sedums and other small perennial plants of her terrarium home.

to shade and back to keep from becoming too hot (*hyperthermous*) or too cold (*hypothermous*). The color displayed by an anole is one indication of the temperature state of the animal—bright green indicates warm, grey-brown indicates cold.

The anole is rapid in its movement. One reason for this is that the animal must be fast enough to catch insects in flight. Another reason is that fast motion helps to stabilize or steady its body temperature. The

Illus. 19. The remarkable head of the anole with its organs of smell, sight, and sound lying distributed along the horizontal line of its head. (Enlarged photo.)

1. Ear opening (sound). 2. Eye (sight). 3. Nostril (smell).

anole's head is held up, above its shoulders, and the major sense organs are set in a horizontal line along both sides of the head (Illus. 19 and 20).

Even when the eye is closed to ward off the sunlight as in an afternoon snooze, the keen senses of hearing (which can also detect vibrations) and smell are active and alert.

Eyes

The skull of the anole is light and strong in construction, similar to other lizards and to birds. It is

26

Illus. 20. The arrow-shaped head of a mature anole has separately focusing eyes, one on each side of the head, in order to survey the widest possible territory. (Enlarged photo.)

1. Eye.

equipped with huge eye sockets and a set of backward-curving teeth for seizing and crushing its insect victims (Illus. 21, 22 and 23).

The eye has the lizard characteristic of a nearly clear lens, and is supplied with yellow oil droplets which filter out the longer wavelengths of light. The lens is round and the position of the eyes provides for only about 15° of binocular vision—the overlap of the field of vision of both eyes. (In human vision, the overlap is far higher.) This lack of large-scale binocular vision allows the anole spectacular side and rear vision. The

Illus. 21. An enlargement of the anole skull of a large, mature male.

1. Light, but strong bones of the skull reduce weight and allow for quick bird-like movements.
2. Rearward slanting teeth.
3. Long, narrow dentary bone.
4. Nostril opening.
5. Very large eye socket.

anole is able to catch sight of insects moving in its field of view at a distance of 7.5 metres (25 feet) at right angles to its body. It can detect a member of its own species at even greater distances.

Illus. 22. The anole eye looks directly into the camera.

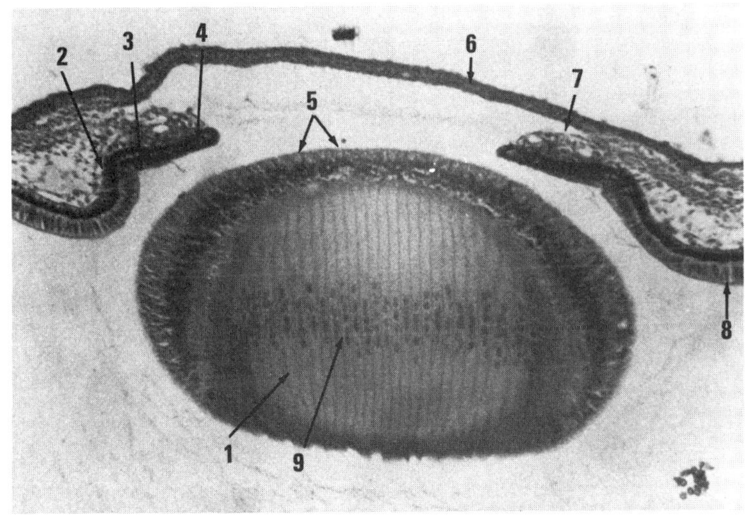

Illus. 23. Microphotograph of section of eye.

1. Fibre-tracts of clear lens. 2. Ciliary muscle. 3. Sphincter. 4. Dilatator. 5. Iris. 6. Cornea. 7. Canal of Schlemm. 8. Ciliary body. 9. Nuclei of cells.

Illus. 24. The underside of the head reveals an intricate pattern of scales.

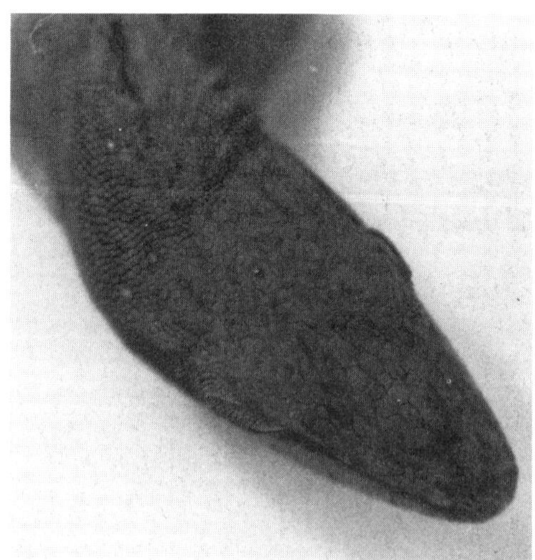

Illus. 25. View of top or dorsal surface of anole head.

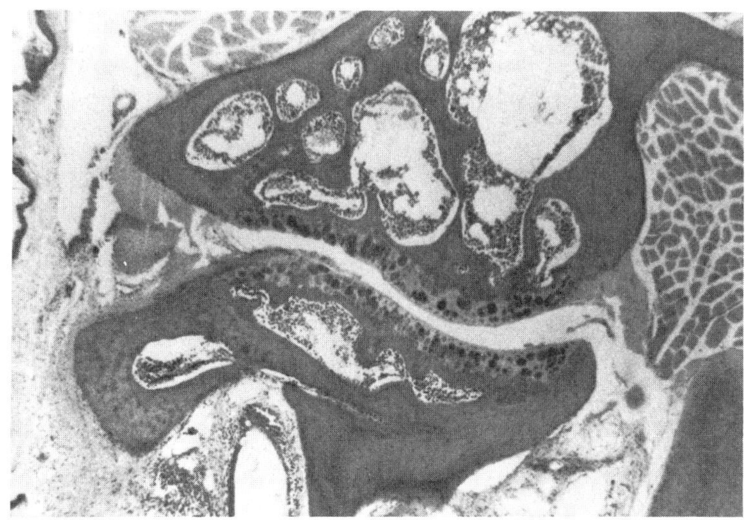

Illus. 26. Microphotograph of section through ear of anole.

Ears

The ears serve as both organs of hearing and organs of equilibrium, or sense of balance. The hearing of anoles is well developed. Their ears are visible on the sides of the head towards the rear, as small holes with no external parts. The ear drum lies just a few millimetres inside the opening (Illus. 25 and 26).

Internal Anatomy

The internal anatomy of the anole is simple and well worth examining. Prepared specimens for classroom dissection can be purchased inexpensively from bio-

Illus. 27. The features of the underside of a mature anole.

Illus. 28. Back view
of a mature female
anole shows
placement of the
eyes.

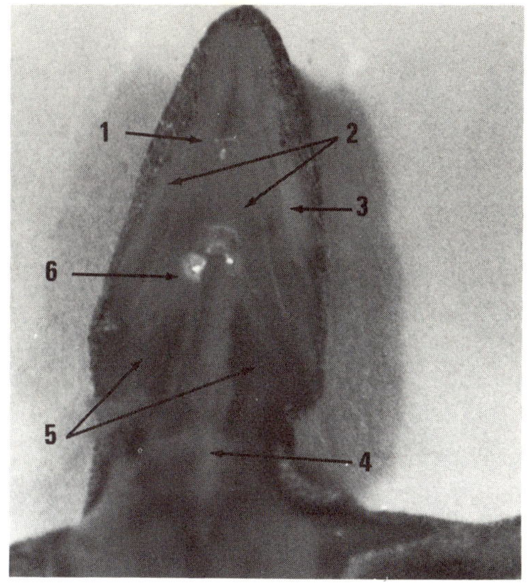

Illus. 29. The underside of the head and neck with the skin stripped back to show major muscles of the lower jaw and head.

1. Geniohyoid muscle (aids in depressing lower jaw).
2. Intermandibular muscles (raise and lower floor of the mouth in swallowing and breathing).
3. Superficial fascia (connective tissue).
4. Coracoid cartilage.
5. Hyoid muscles (depress lower jaw).
6. Esophagus under this muscle and cartilage.

logical supply companies. The major internal systems—muscular, digestive, glandular and reproductive—are shown in detail in Illus. 29 through 46.

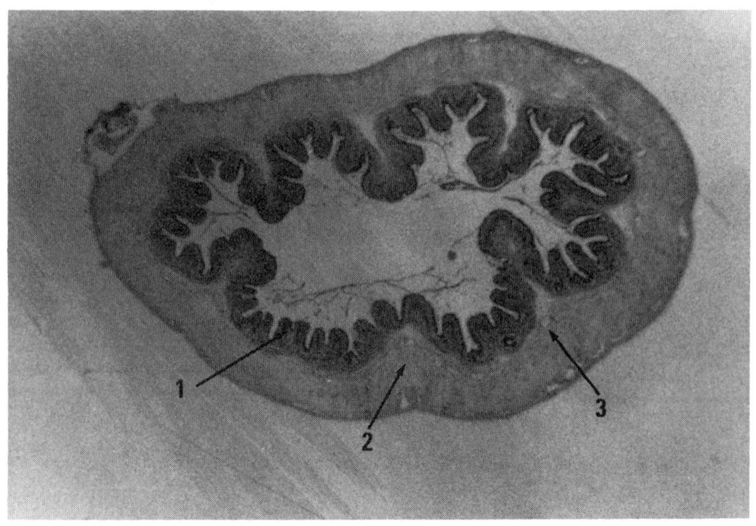

Illus. 30. Microphotograph of cross-section of esophagus.

1. Epithelial cells for producing secretions for starting digestion.
2. Muscular walls for swallowing.
3. Blood vessel.

The internal anatomy of the anole is characteristic of a fast-moving, poilikothermous animal dependent on a high-protein diet of insects. The upper or dorsal surface of the anole body does not have very many visible anatomical features other than the vertebrae

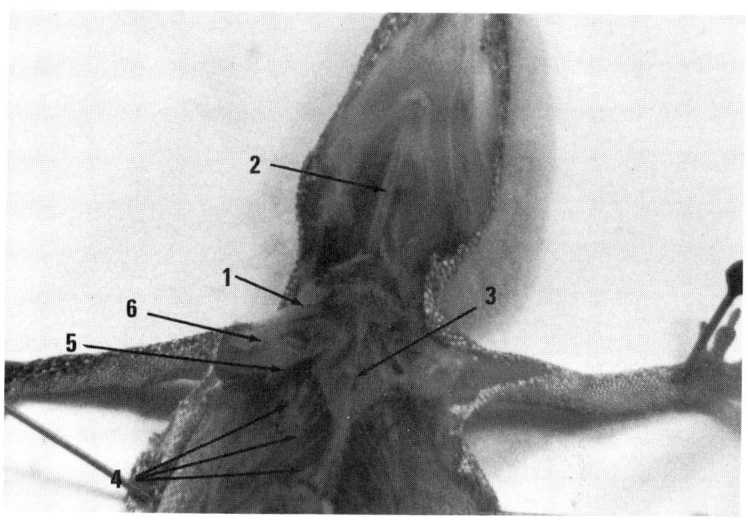

Illus. 31. The underside of the shoulders and upper chest, skin stripped
back to show major muscles of the fore limbs.

1. Humerus muscle (pulls limb forward).
2. This cartilage raises and lowers the throat fan or "dewlap."
3. Pectoral muscle (pulls fore limbs in towards the body).
4. Abdominal muscles.
5. Coracobrachial muscle (pulls limb backwards).
6. Antebrachial muscle (moves the elbow).

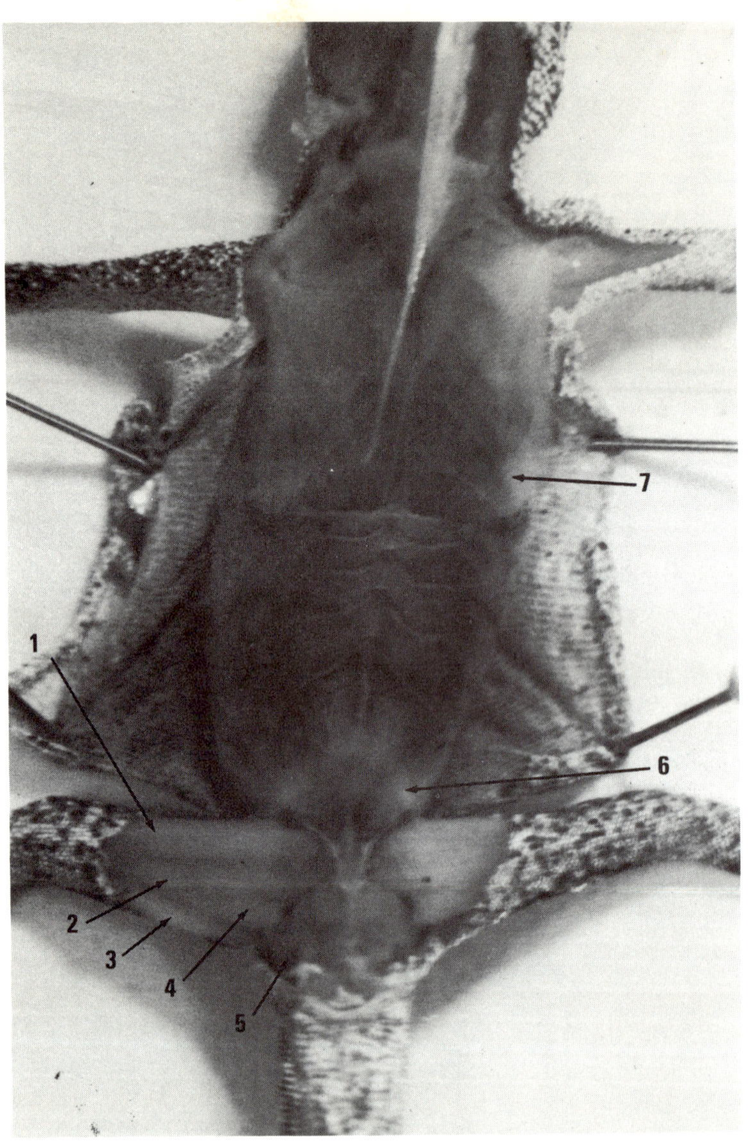

Illus. 32. The underside of the back legs and tail, skin stripped back to show major muscles of the hind limbs.

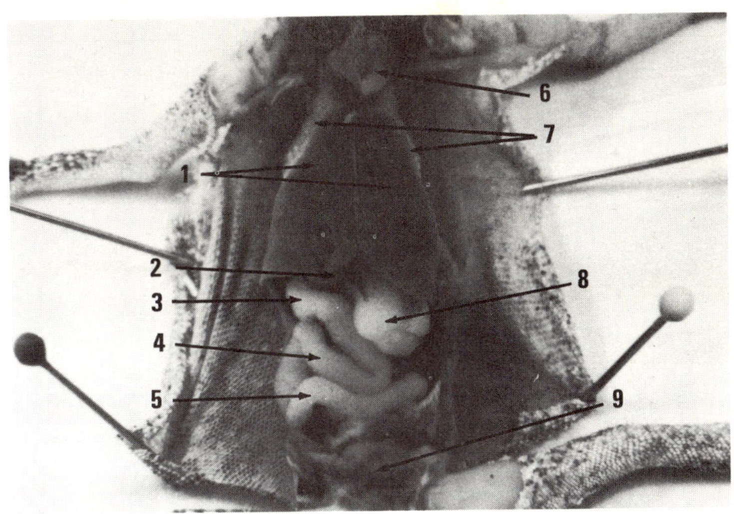

Illus. 33. The internal digestive organs of a large male anole.

1. Liver lobes. 2. Gall bladder. 3. Upper intestinal tract (small). 4. Mid-intestine. 5. Large intestine. 6. Pericardial sac (heart within). 7. Edges of lungs. 8. Stomach. 9. Cloaca (beneath muscles).

(Opposite page) 1. Pubo-ischio-femoral internal muscle (pulls hind limb forwards).
  2. Pubo-tibial muscle (helps to pull limb forward).
  3. Ischio-flexoral muscle (spreads knee and toes).
  4. Part of the pubo-ischio-tibial muscle (spreads and extends the knee).
  5. Ischio-caudal and caudo-cruval muscles (move the tail).
  6. Pubo-ischio-femoral muscles (pull the main leg bone forward).
  7. External oblique muscles.

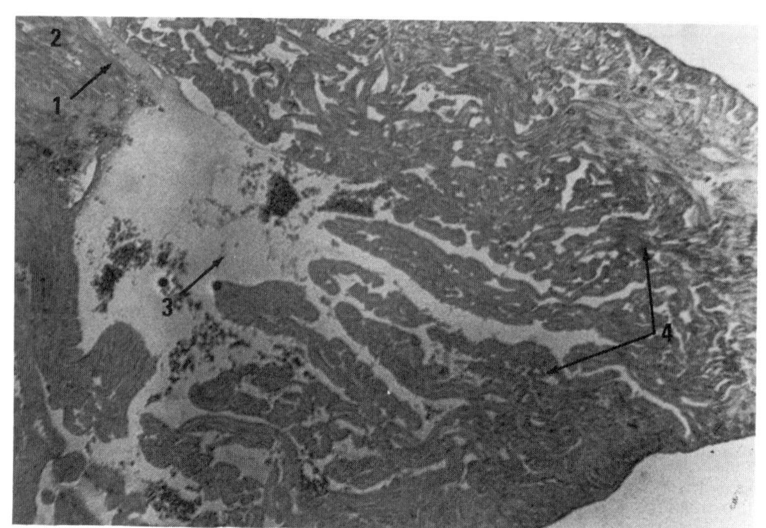

Illus. 34. Microphotograph of vertical section of the heart.

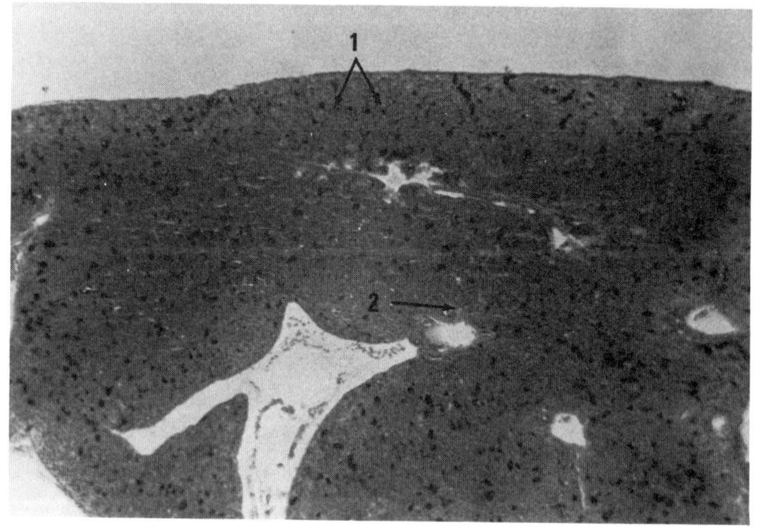

Illus. 35. Microphotograph of section through the liver.

38

Illus. 36. Micro-
photograph of
vertical section of
stomach.

1. Epithelial cells.
2. Muscular wall of
   stomach.

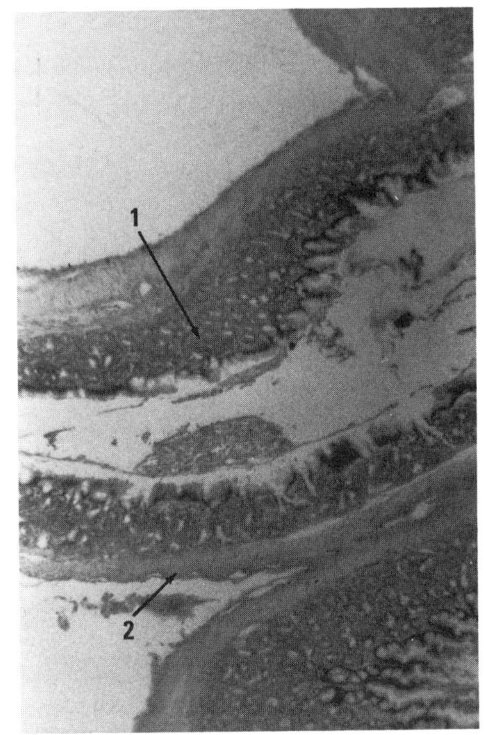

(Opposite page, top)

1. Part of septum which divides the chambers.
2. Aorta.
3. Dorsal chamber.
4. Heart muscle.

(Opposite page, bottom)

1. Cords of liver cells.
2. Bile duct.

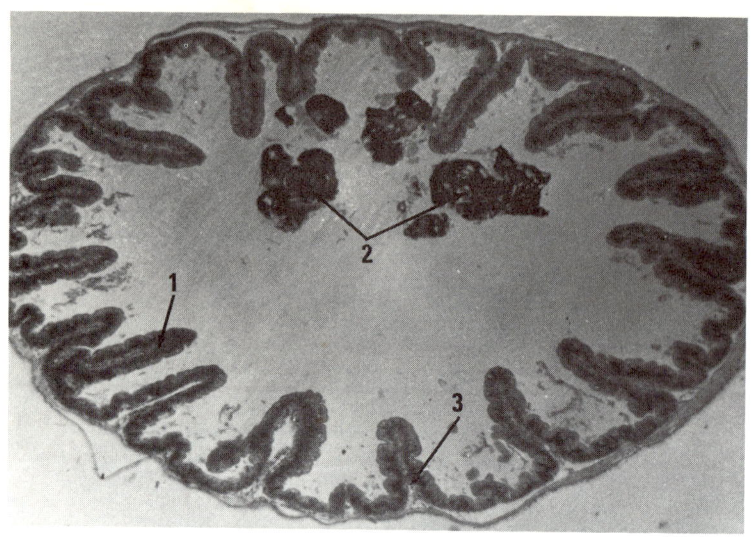

Illus. 37. Microphotograph of cross-section of upper or small intestine.

1. Villi. 2. Food particles. 3. Blood cells carrying away digested food.

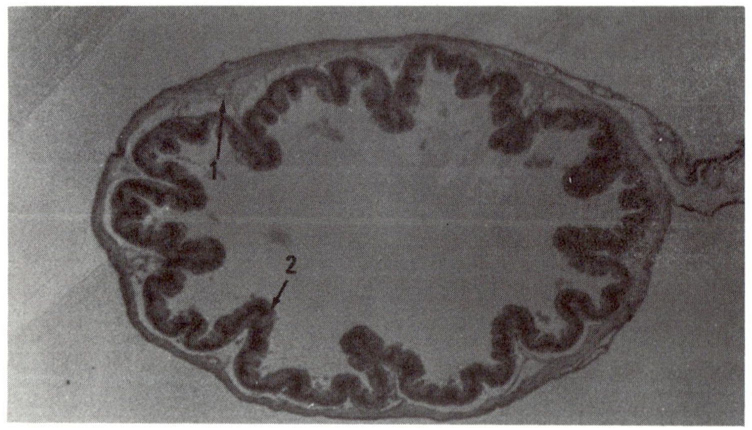

Illus. 38. Microphotograph of cross-section through middle of intestine.

1. Blood vessel. 2. Villi.

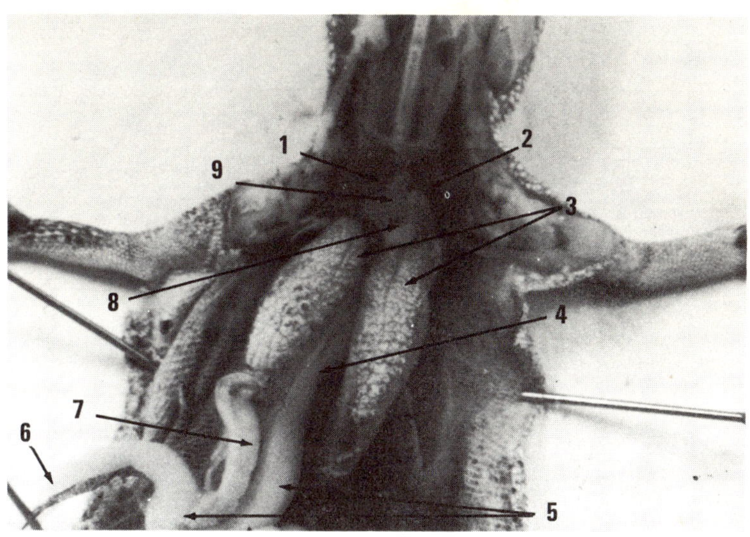

Illus. 39. Internal organs of a large male anole with liver removed to show lungs and heart.

1. Right atrium of heart.
2. Left atrium of heart.
3. Lungs.
4. Esophagus.
5. Stomach.
6. Loop of small intestine.
7. Pancreas.
8. Postcava (hepatic sinus of heart).
9. Ventricle of heart.

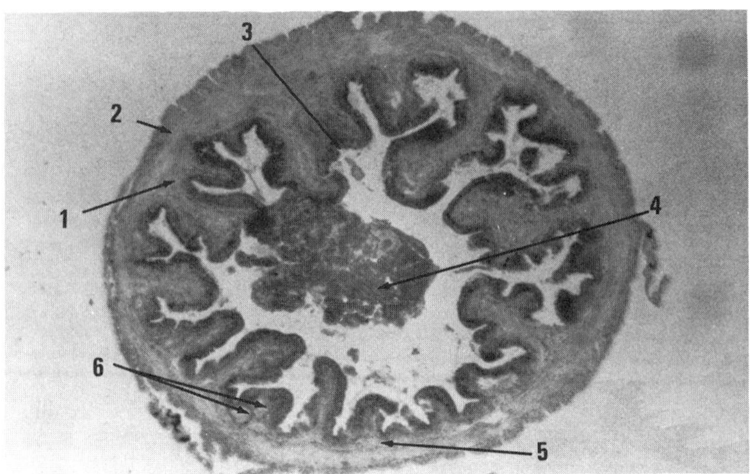

Illus. 40. Microphotograph of cross-section through large intestine.

1. Muscular compactor cells.
2. Longitudinal muscle.
3. Water-extracting cells.
4. Food and waste.
5. Circular muscle.
6. Glandular cells.

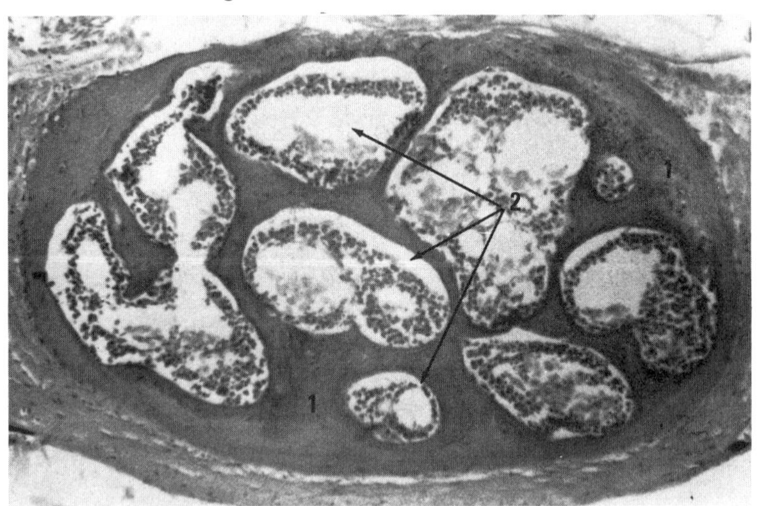

Illus. 41. Spinal column showing vertebra and marrow.

1. Bone. 2. Marrow and blood cells.

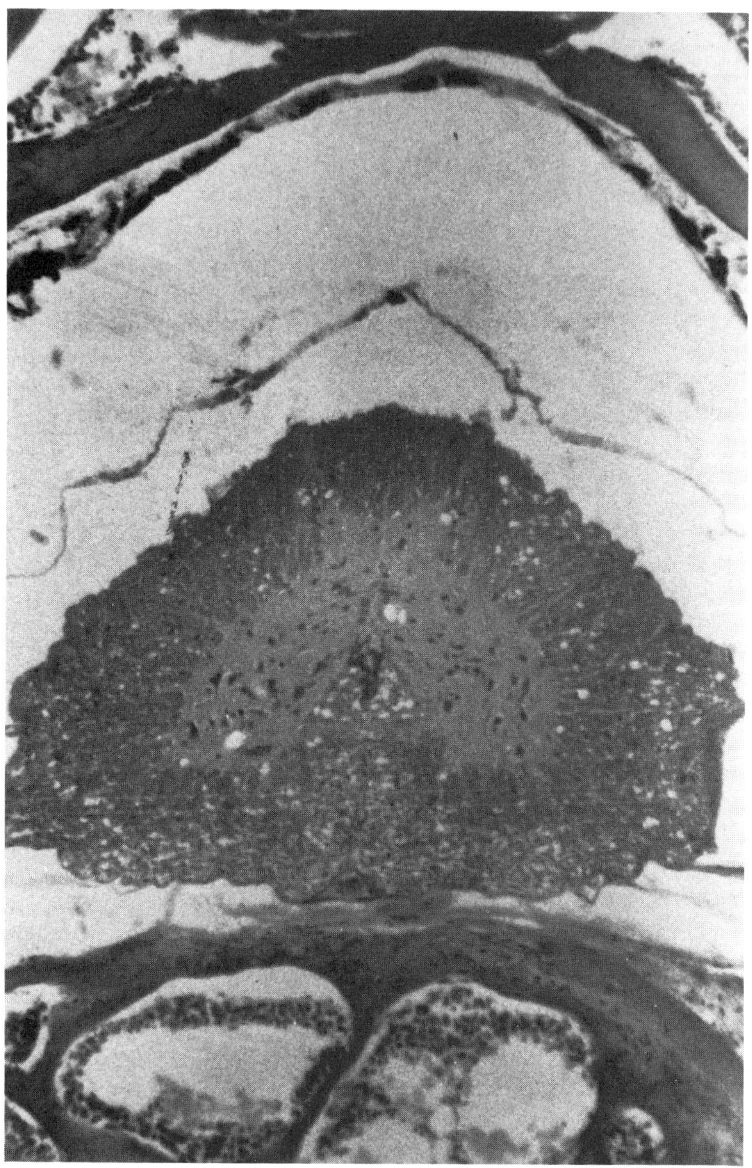

Illus. 42. Microphotograph of cross-section of spinal chord.

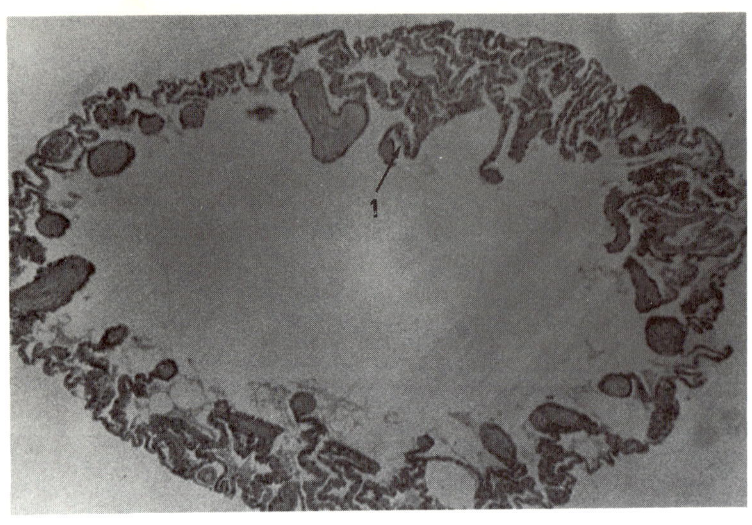

Illus. 43. Microphotograph of cross-section of lung.

1. Tubes to increase surface area of lung.

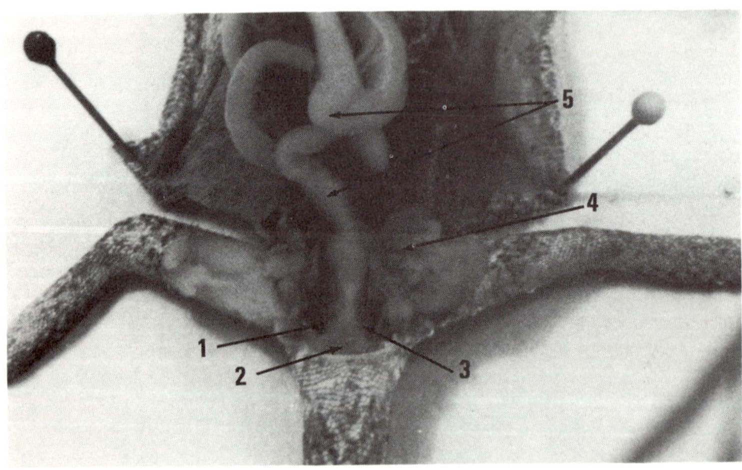

Illus. 44. The lower digestive tract of a large male anole.

1. Cloaca. 2. Anal pore. 3. Postcava (vein). 4. Testis. 5. Large intestine

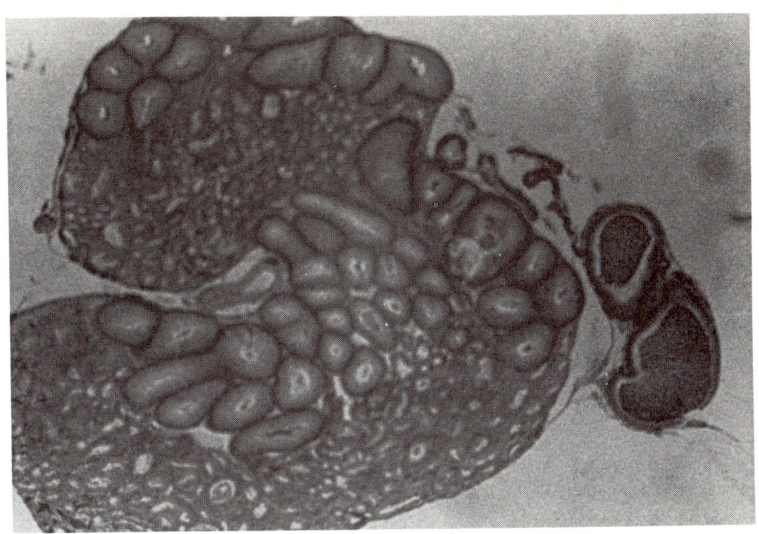

Illus. 45. Cross-section of the kidney.

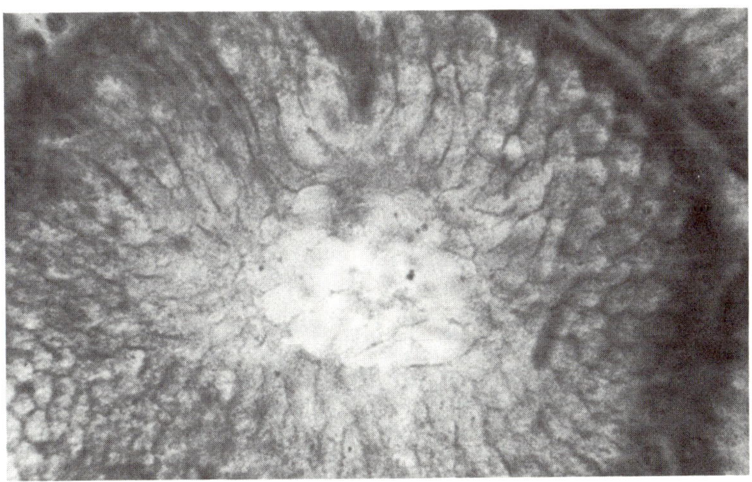

Illus. 46. A highly magnified microphotograph of one of the tubules of the kidney in which filtration of nitrogen-loaded wastes is accomplished.

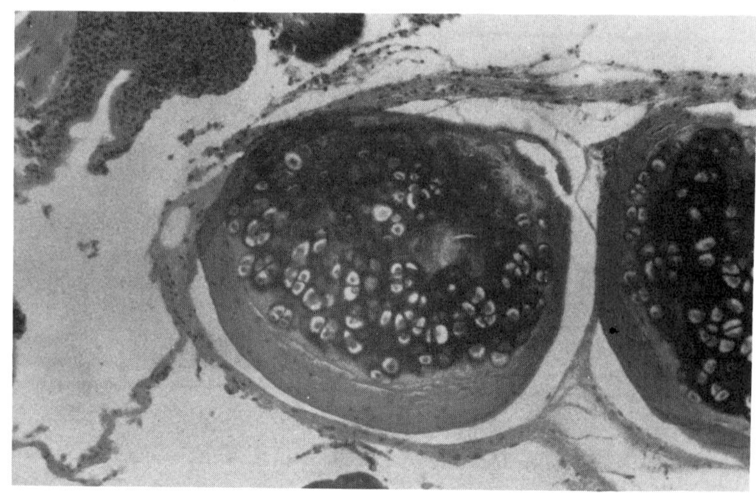

Illus. 47. A highly magnified microphotograph of a major blood vessel showing the large number of blood cells crowded between the walls.

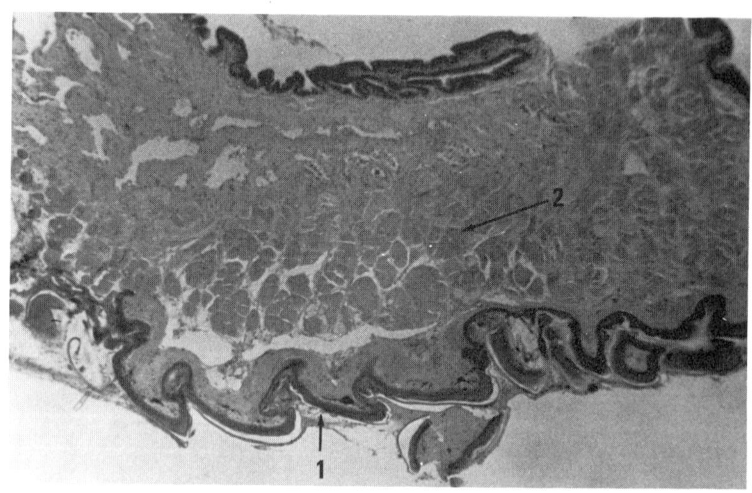

Illus. 48. Microphotograph of vertical section of cloaca.

1. Scales and skin. 2. Cellular lining of cloaca.

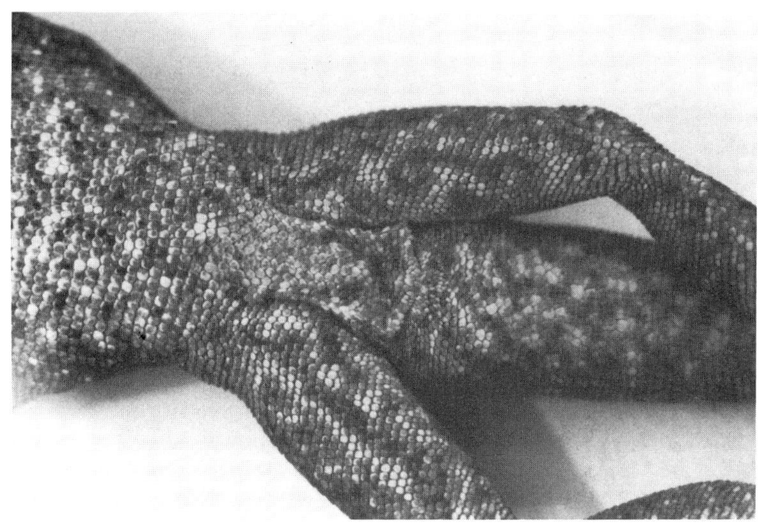

Illus. 49. The pelvic region and tail attachment.

and muscles. The lower or ventral surface reveals many features such as the neck muscles, ribs and the vent or cloacal opening. The vent or cloaca is an opening in reptiles, amphibians and birds into which the genital, urinary and intestinal organs all discharge (Illus. 48).

Examination of the underside of an anole will also show that its legs are really attached at the sides of the pelvis rather than under the body as in a dog, rabbit or other mammal. This placement of the limbs causes the anole to crawl or appear to ''swim'' over the ground (Illus. 49).

The Skin

The skin and scales of the anole are one of its most important adaptations. The skin, which is leathery and flexible, forms a strong but pliable covering over the whole body (Illus. 50 and 51).

There are tracts of darker and lighter color, often seen as faint stripes covering the whole of the skin. The dominant color pattern is a counter shaded effect.

Illus. 51. The individual blotches of lighter and darker color can be intensified or reduced adding to the protective coloration.

This means that the upper part of the anole from the tip of its snout to the distal or end portion of its tail is dark, ranging in color from a bright, vibrant green through a grey-blue to a dark chocolate brown. The underside, however, stays a pinkish white or cream. This renders the animal dark when seen from above and light like the sky when seen from underneath while resting on a branch or climbing a tree or vine (Illus. 53).

Illus. 53. Countershading tends to disguise an anole in its habitat, in this case, some garden plants.

1. Dark on top. 2. Light underneath.

The Tail

The tail is an important part of the body, since it is a balancing organ that aids the anole in running and climbing and also since it stores water and food in the form of fat for the winter hibernation. The tail does not change color as rapidly or intensely as the rest of the anole's body (Illus. 54). It is covered with a dense

50

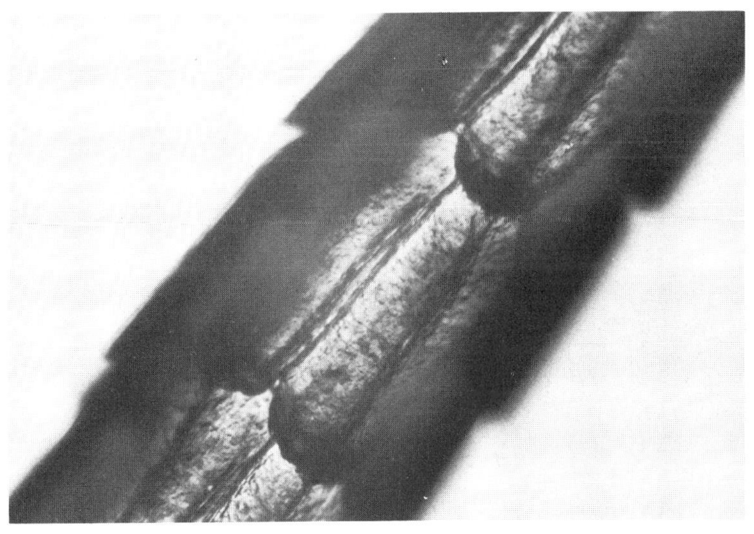

Illus. 54. The anole's tail is usually a solid and slightly brighter color than the rest of the lizard. Here the lizard rests on some bright green leaves.

Illus. 55. A highly magnified view of the tail scales.

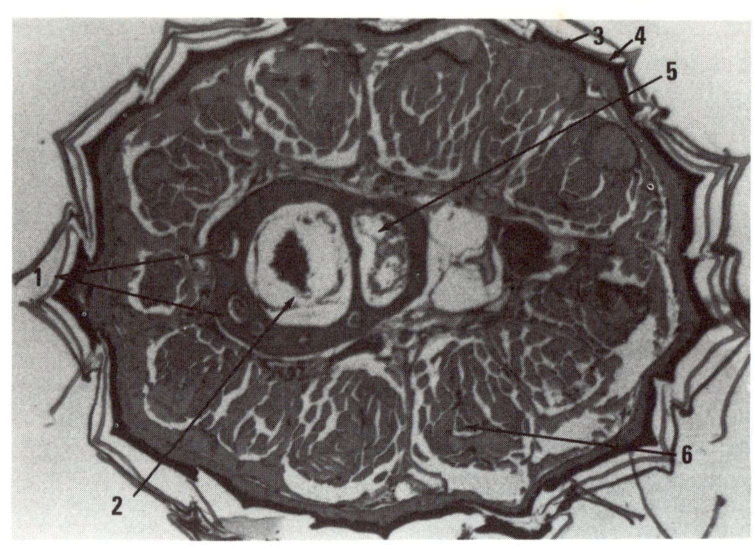

Illus. 56. Microphotograph of a cross-section through the tail near the base.

1. Blood vessels. 2. Spinal cord. 3. Scale. 4. Skin. 5. Vertebra. 6. Muscle.

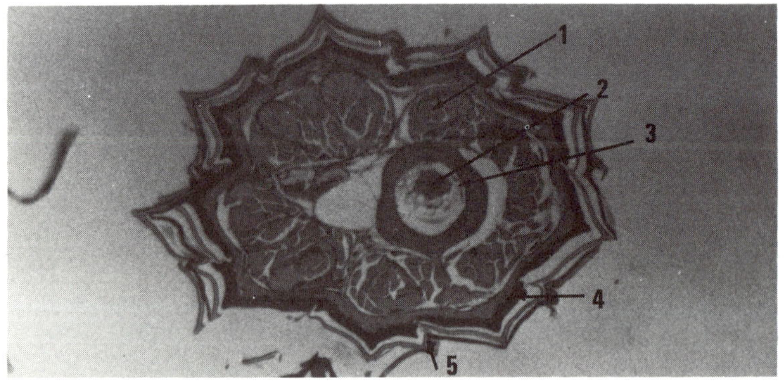

Illus. 57. Microphotograph of a cross-section near the tip of the tail.

1. Muscle. 2. Spinal cord. 3. Vertebra. 4. Scale. 5. Skin.

layer of interlocking scales like the armor of a medieval knight (Illus. 55). A microscopic cross-section shows it to be a "coaxial cable" of bone, muscle and nerve (Illus. 56 and 57).

Regeneration

Lizards are famous for their ability to shed their tails and later regenerate them. When pursued by a predator, the lizard sheds its tail, which then twitches inde-

Illus. 59. A highly magnified view of the skin on the back.

pendently and thus distracts the enemy. While the anole can lose its tail, it requires more effort to do so than with some other lizards. If the end of the tail (the last 1.25 centimetres or ½ inch) is dropped off, the anole can regenerate some of it. The new tail growth will appear at the next shed or moult, when the lizard casts its skin. The reason for this is the outer coating of the anole is dead tissue. The skin is flexible but it will not grow, so that the anole frequently outgrows its skin. When this happens, the skin splits around the neck and shoulders and peels down the back all the way to the tail. The skin of the back is the thickest and has plates something like the tiles on a roof (Illus. 59).

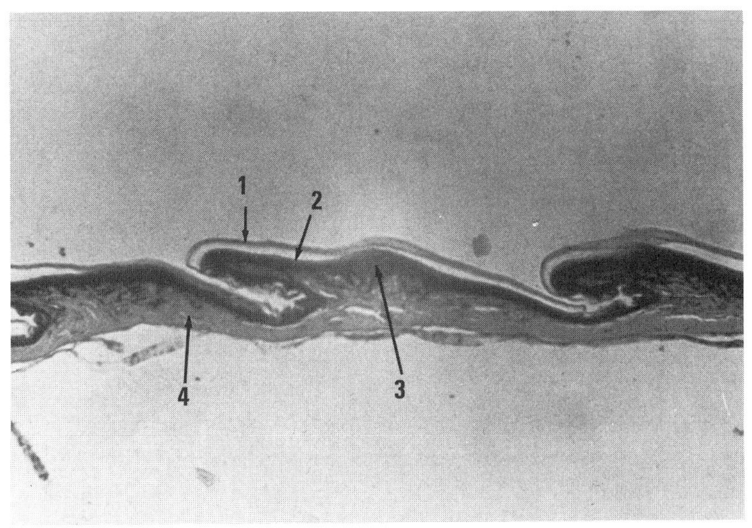

Illus. 60. Microphotograph of cross-section of skin.

1. Outermost skin. 2. Hard scale. 3. Pigment cell (chromatophores).
4. Superficial muscle and blood supply.

Color Change

The color change of the anole takes place in the color-bearing cells or *chromatophores*, branching, tree-like cells which lie directly under the transparent scales. They expand and turn the animal darker when affected by a hormone, a chemical substance secreted by the pituitary gland which lies close to the brain. As the hormone flows through the circulatory system it causes the individual chromatophores to expand. The

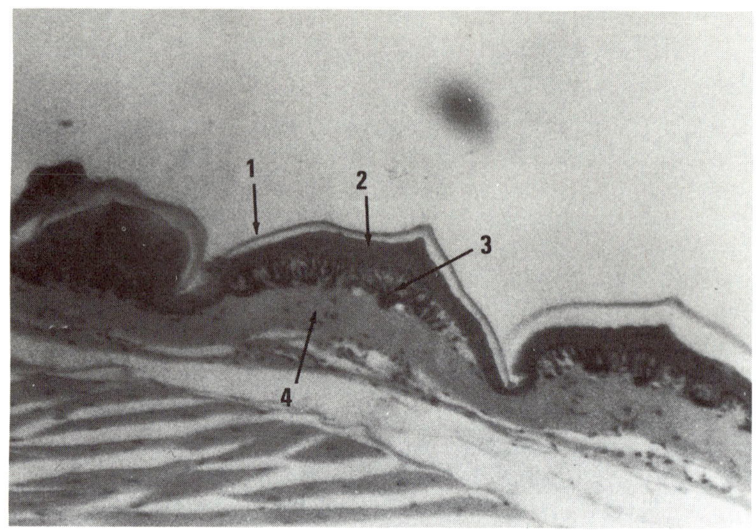

Illus. 61. Microphotograph of vertical section of skin. Note expansion of black extensions or branches of the chromatophores, specimen in brown color state.

1. Outermost skin.
2. Hard scale.
3. Pigment cell (chromatophores).
4. Superficial muscle and blood supply.

effect is to turn the entire upper surface from green to brown. The complete process of turning color takes about five minutes. However, the change from green to brown is quicker than that from brown to green. The change of color can be influenced by heat, light and the irritability of the anole but it is not under the conscious control of the animal (Illus. 60 and 61).

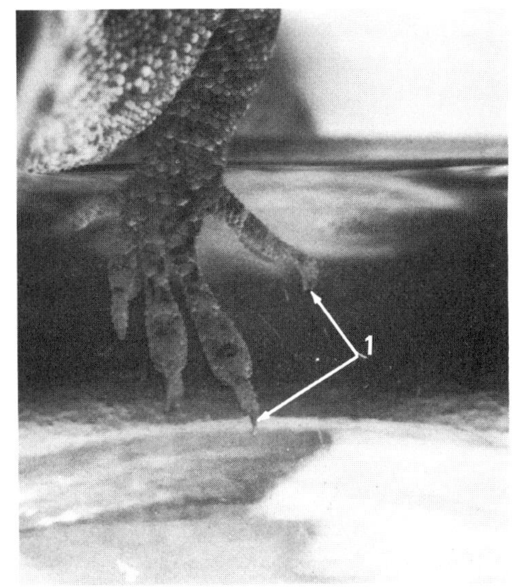

Illus. 62. The upper surface of the anole fore limb shows the wide toe and claw.

1. Claws.

The Limbs

The limbs of the anole are adapted for a nearly complete arboreal, or tree-climbing, existence. Anoles are only rarely found above three metres (10 feet) from the ground and rarely actually on the ground, since they are usually climbing over plants and shrubs. The front or fore limb has small curved claws and adhesive pads to the rear of the claws. This double set of climbing apparatus enables the anole to climb far and fast over natural surfaces, such as tree bark and leaves, as well as over man-made surfaces such as windows and walls. The anole is not a great jumper and

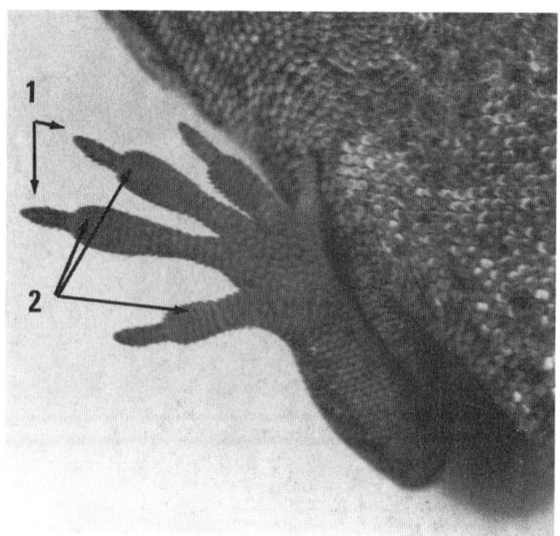

Illus. 63. The lower surface of the fore limb shows the broad sticky pads which enable the anole to run up vertical sheets of glass and over walls.

1. Claws.
2. Adhesive pads.

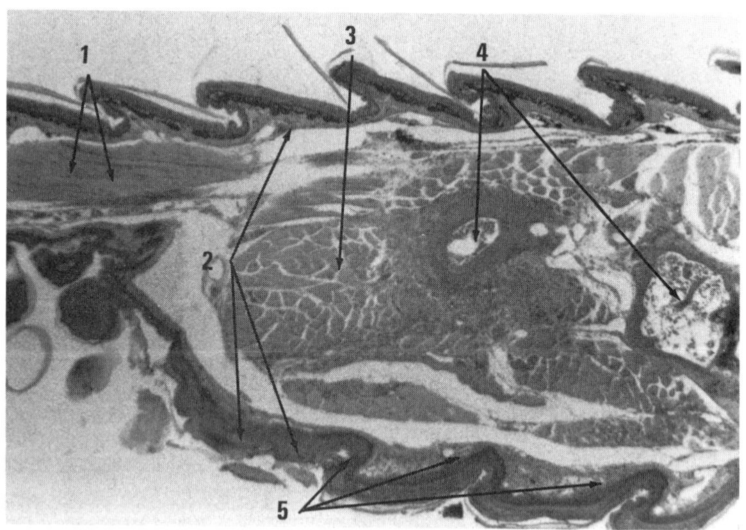

Illus. 64. A low-power microphotograph of a section through the toe of an anole.

1. Connection at knuckles. 2. Scales. 3. Muscle. 4. Bone. 5. Adhesive pad area.

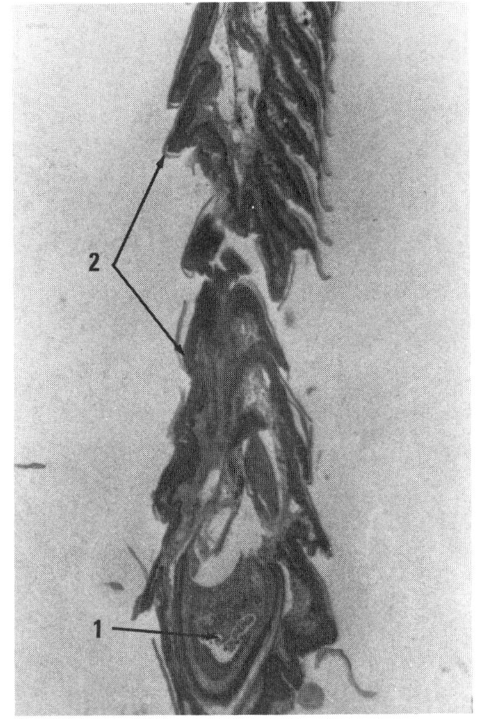

Illus. 65. Micro-photograph of section through longer toe bone.

1. Muscle and bone of joint.
2. Scales.

will restrict its leaps to less than a metre (3 feet). Yet it will often fall out of trees or other high perches during mating battles with no ill effects (Illus. 62, 63, 64, 65 and 66).

The hind limb is held close to the body and used to push the body forward when the fore limb has been extended. It has larger claws and larger adhesive pads (Illus. 67 and 68). The hind limbs are never used for

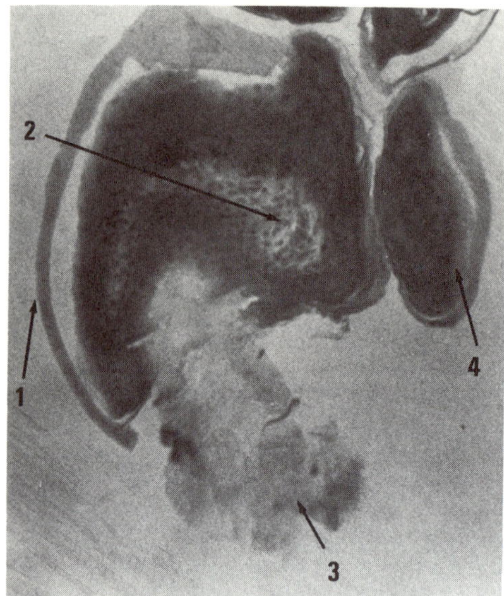

Illus. 66. High power microphotograph showing distal (farthest) tip of toe with covering scale and claw.

1. Toe nail scale.
2. Muscle.
3. Claw.
4. Toe pad.

Illus. 67. The anole usually keeps the knee bent and the hind limbs ready for instant springing, for the capture of food or to make a quick getaway.

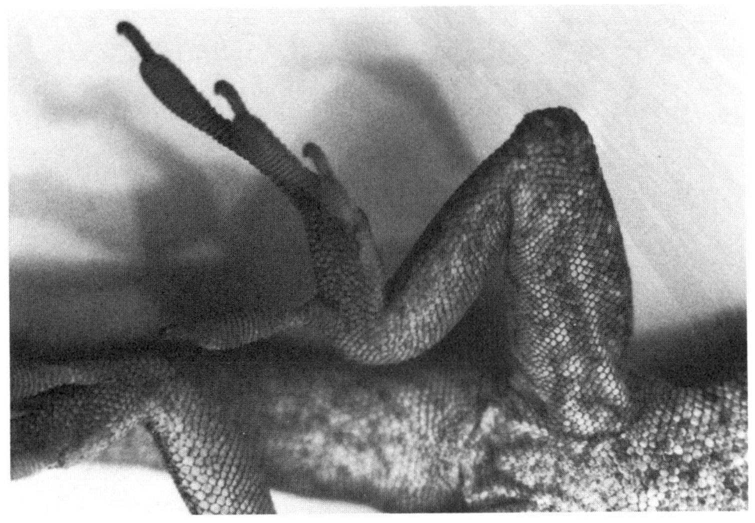

Illus. 68. A close-up of the powerful hind limb from beneath showing its backward-curving claws.

capturing food, unlike the jaws and fore limbs, which may both aid in the seizure of insects. The limbs, color change and acute sense organs fit the anole well for its life cycle.

Illus. 69. A pregnant female anole looks for places to lay her eggs.

4. LIFE CYCLE IN NATURE AND CAPTIVITY

The anole comes out of its winter hibernation about the middle of February in its most northern range. It begins immediately to feed on the clouds of insects breeding over most of its territory. The anoles mate and the females lay their eggs in shallow holes in the soft ground (Illus. 69). Anole nests are often found in and around the roots of garden plants where the soil is cultivated and easily dug.

Mating Cycle

During the summer days, the anoles eat away at the wide variety of flying and swarming insects. The large bugs and flies are especially tempting and after a good meal the well-stuffed anoles doze in the sun. As the weather warms up, and the sun climbs higher in the sky it affects the breeding cycles of the anole. The male testes increase the production of sperm with the rise of the sun until the summer solstice (June 21 in the northern hemisphere). This association of the anole breeding cycle with the sun's cycle is called *photo-*

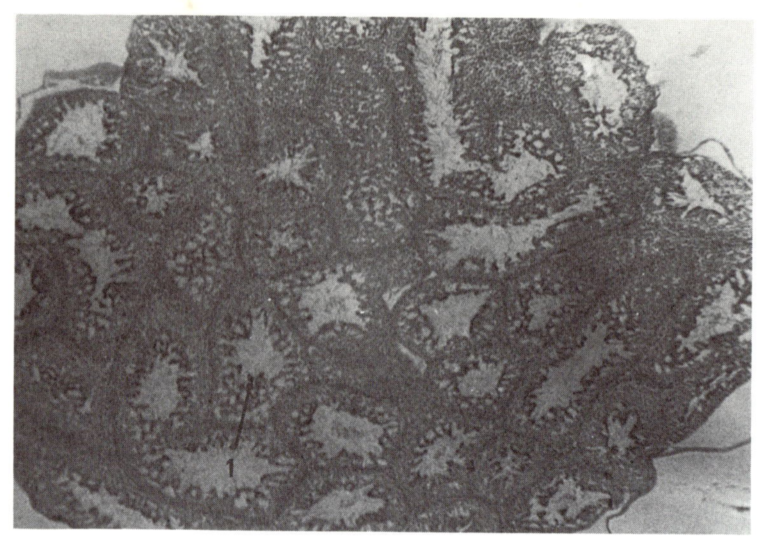

Illus. 70. Microphotograph of section of testes.

1. Sperm developing in testes.

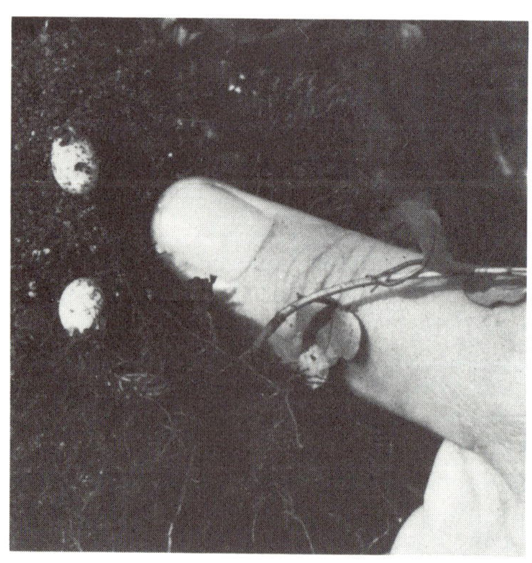

Illus. 71. A clutch
of anole eggs have
been found a few
centimetres (one
inch) below the
roots of a plant.

periodism. Photoperiodism affects the eyes, the pituitary and the reproductive system.

It has been discovered that the female anole possesses special sperm receptacles which can keep sperm alive for up to six months. Therefore females may lay eggs for months or a whole season after mating. Some females probably lay spring eggs after mating the previous autumn. These additional reproductive adaptations add greatly to the anole's competitive edge in its environment.

The Eggs

The eggs are roughly oval and about 1.7 cm ($\frac{11}{16}$ inch) in length (Illus. 71).

Illus. 72. The eggs have been carefully transferred to a reptile incubator.

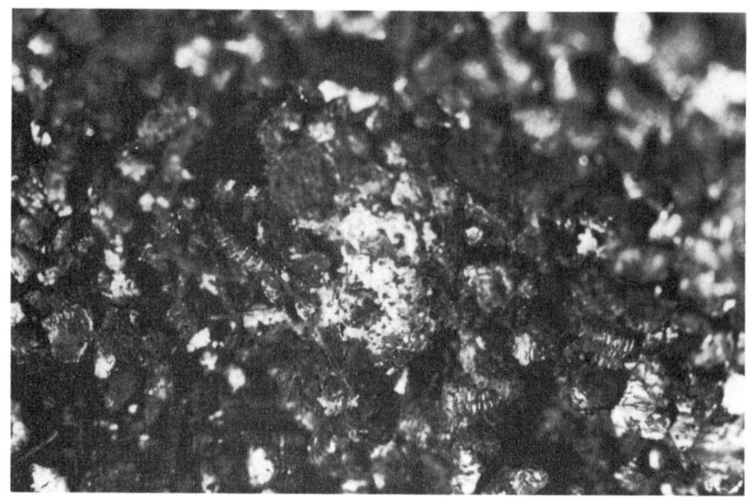

Illus. 73. A gentle shake covers the egg with the mixture of dry vermiculite and damp potting soil.

They are slightly leathery to the touch and usually just a bit sticky from a lubricant secreted by the female's body. Although the eggs are white in color, this is not always apparent, since the lubricant allows fine particles of earth to stick to them.

If anole eggs are found in the garden they should be moved to a reptile incubator. This can be any type of glass container, a gallon jug (3.8 litres), a quart jar (0.95 litres) or a glass dish of at least 8 cm depth ($3\frac{1}{4}$ inch). This container should be filled to a depth of 6 cm ($2\frac{1}{2}$ inches) with dry vermiculite with about 1/10th of clean, sterile potting soil mixed in.

This potting soil should be of the commercial type that has been cleaned to remove insect grubs and small

Illus. 74. Once a week the soil is shaken from the grainy white eggs and they are sprinkled with tepid water from a small eye-dropper or pipette.

beetles which might damage the eggs. Lift the eggs carefully with a clean spoon or forceps. They should not be touched with the fingers as this may transfer bacteria or viruses from the skin to the egg. Also the pressure needed to pick up a slightly slippery egg with the fingers may damage it.

Place the eggs on the bed of vermiculite and give the whole container a quick but short shake. This will just cover the eggs with a fine layer of vermiculite (Illus. 72). The top of the container should have holes or slots to permit the interchange of air. Once a week a few drops of clean, not distilled, water should be sprinkled over the eggs. Every other week, the covered eggs should be shaken clean so that any that have fungus or have dried up can be removed. As the eggs develop, they should remain round and full and swell slightly throughout their development (Illus. 73 and 74).

Structure of the Egg

The egg is a completely self-contained liquid environment, a total life-support system as complete and complex as any space capsule. It provides a watery environment for the full development of the embryo of a basically aquatic animal far from any pond or stream. The anole egg is fairly large and perfect as a sample of the basic reptile egg for study.

The egg is mostly a jelly-like mass of foodstuff. The embryo develops through all of its embryonic stages as a sort of thick layer of microscopic cells on one small surface section of the enormous yolk. This marvelous egg has a tough outer covering which resists physical jolts and also prying by insects and other predatory invertebrates. The large yolk provides a long-range food supply so that the young anole hatches out ready to seek its own food without any intermediate period of development.

If the anole young is compared to the newly hatched tadpole, it is obvious that the slow moving tadpole, which is completely dependent on water for its

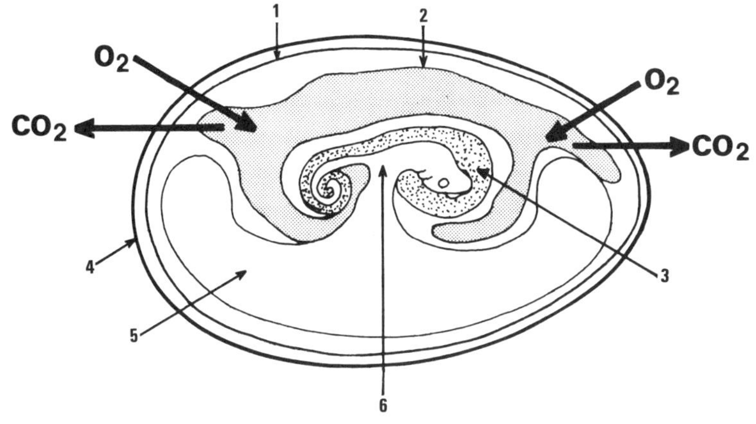

Diagram A: 1. Chorion. 2. Allantois. 3. Amnion and amniotic sac. 4. Shell. 5. Embryo. 6. Yolk.

habitat and low-nutriment algae for its food, is not nearly as ready to compete in life with the swift-moving, variably colored anole which can live on land or swim in water and eat high-protein insects.

Inside the anole egg are three incredible membranes, each a thin, flexible, skin-like sheet of cells which has a specific purpose and serves a definite function (Diagram A). The first membrane inside the egg shell is the *chorion*, which lines the shell and aids in protecting both the embryo and the yolk. The second is a permeable membrane through which oxygen passes into the embryo and carbon dioxide passes out. This,

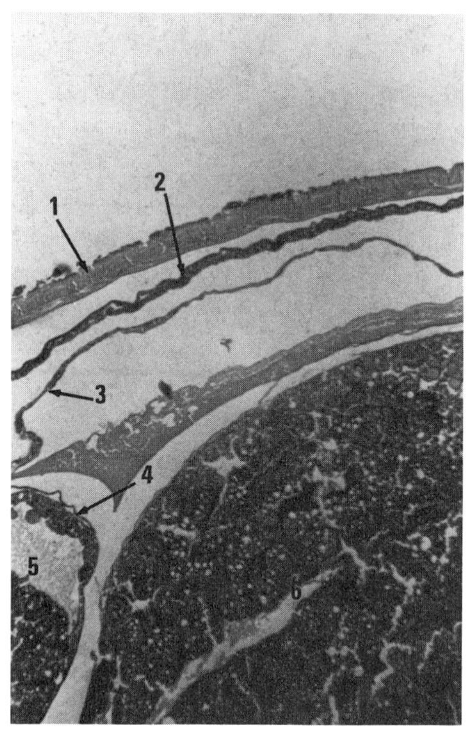

Illus. 75. Micro-photograph of section through egg.

1. Egg shell.
2. Chorion.
3. Allantois.
4. Amnion.
5. Embryo.
6. Yolk.

called the *allantois*, acts as a lung and aids in the elimination of nitrogen wastes. These wastes build up as the embryo digests and forms or synthesizes proteins. They are very poisonous but are combined with other chemicals to form harmless compounds. The anole eliminates its nitrogen waste as a thick white paste similar to bird droppings and not as liquid urine, like mammals.

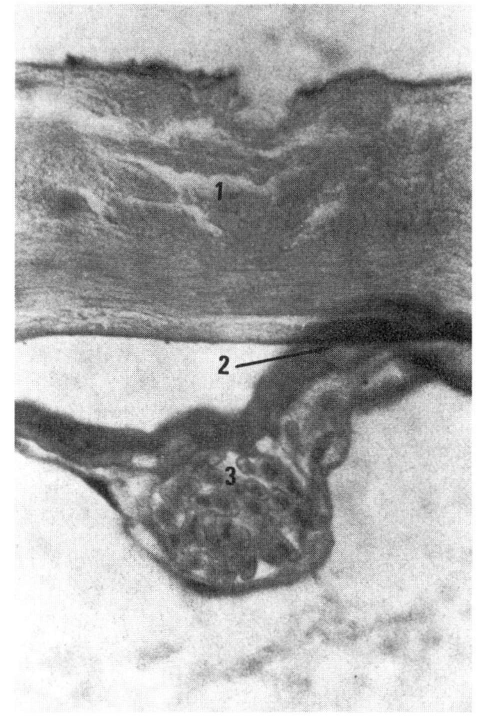

Illus. 76. High power microphotograph of small section of egg.

1. Egg shell.
2. Chorion.
3. Blood vessel.

The innermost membrane is the *amnion*. This membrane completely encloses the embryo in liquid, serving as a miniature pond or aquarium although the egg may be miles from such water. The amnion supplies a synthetic environment, a life support system just as the space capsule provides a tiny container of earth atmosphere and temperature in the hostile regions of space (Illus. 75, 76, 77 and 78).

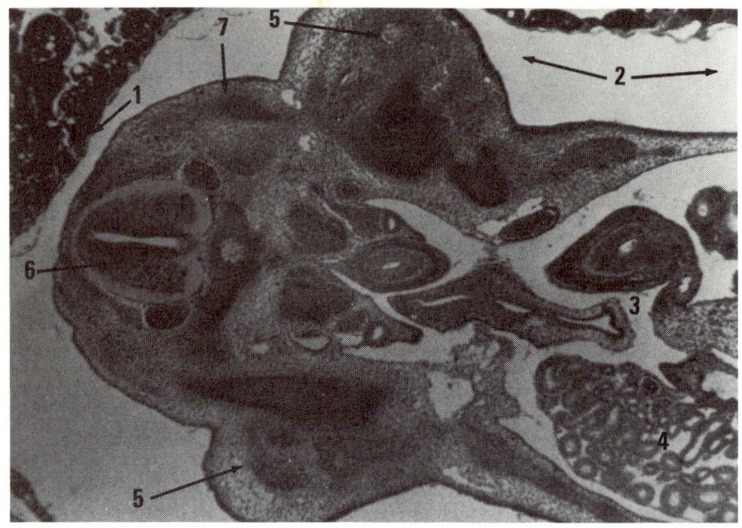

Illus. 77. Low-power microphotograph of sagittal (midpoint) section through egg and well developed embryo.

1. Amnion. 2. Liquid-filled space. 3. Digestive tract. 4. Lungs. 5. Limb buds. 6. Brain. 7. Eye.

The egg develops best at about 29°C (84°F). At this temperature the egg develops and hatches in 70 to 80 days. This is just a little too long a time to escape the cold nights (temperatures below 10°C or 50°F) which occur in the northern edge of its range. The effect of cool temperatures on the development of its egg restricts the anole to the southern United States.

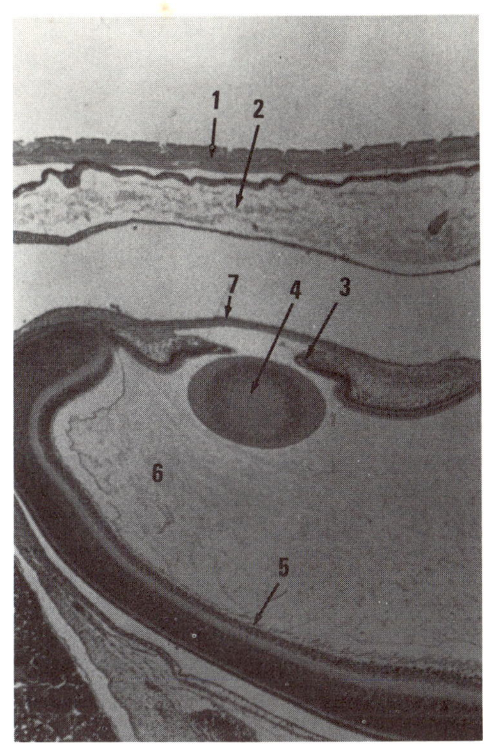

Illus. 78. Micro-photograph of section through eye of embryo.

1. Egg shell.
2. Amnion.
3. Iris.
4. Lens.
5. Retina.
6. Vitreous fluid.
7. Cornea.

The Embryo

The embryo develops in similar fashion to other reptiles and to birds—a very complex process nowhere fully understood as yet. The many organ systems and finely-tuned senses appear and begin to function inside the tiny world of the amnion (Illus. 60) and even the eyes begin to move and twitch long before the tiny anole is ready to hatch (Illus. 78).

Illus. 79. An anole hunts for insects in its plant habitat. It is dark brown as it makes its way from light to shadow.

The Hatchling

As the summer goes by, the small anole grows rapidly. However it will not be old enough to mate until at least the second year. It ceaselessly wanders through the territory in which it hatched, looking for insects. While hunting for food the tiny anoles must stay close to cover as they will be eaten by snakes, shrews and even by larger males of their own species.

Anoles, like some other animals, are not always friendly to their own kind. Half-grown anoles are too big to be devoured by the old males, who will tolerate the presence of half-grown females who have wandered into their territory, but young males old enough to display the throat fan or dewlap are immediately driven out.

Illus. 80. A large male dozes in the sunshine.

CONCLUSION

Remember, the anole is a living creature. It is not an artificial flower or ornament, it cannot be fed over long terms with pieces of meat or commercial pet foods. It will not survive mistreatment. It is a highly organized and sensitive animal, not a plaything or an ornament. Yes, anoles have actually been tethered to the lapels of jackets or pinned up as hair ornaments.

If the anole is kept in spacious quarters with living plants and fed live food it will more than reward its keepers. From the American chameleon a great deal of pleasure and fascination can be derived.

INDEX

Illus. 81. A young female sniffs the air and looks up into the leaves above her for insects.